# How to use this book

*Follow the advice, in italics, given for you on each page.*
*Support the children as they read the text that is shaded in cream.*
**Praise** *the children at every step!*

*Detailed guidance is provided in the Read Write Inc. Phonics Handbook*

## 9 reading activities

*Children:*
*Practise reading the speed sounds.*
*Read the green, red and challenge words for the story.*
*Listen as you read the introduction.*
*Discuss the vocabulary check with you.*
*Read the story.*
*Re-read the story and discuss the 'questions to talk about'.*
*Read the story with fluency and expression.*
*Answer the questions to 'read and answer'.*
*Practise reading the speed words.*

# Speed sounds

**Consonants**  *Say the pure sounds (do not add 'uh').*

| f ff ph | l ll le | m mm | n nn kn | r rr wr | s ss se (c) ce | v ve | z zz se s | sh | th | ng nk |
|---|---|---|---|---|---|---|---|---|---|---|

| b bb | c k ck | d dd | g gg | h | j (g) ge | p pp | qu | t tt | w (wh) | x | y | ch tch |
|---|---|---|---|---|---|---|---|---|---|---|---|---|

**Vowels**  *Say the sounds in and out of order.*

| at | hen head | in | on | up | day make | see tea happy he | high smile lie find | blow home no |
|---|---|---|---|---|---|---|---|---|

| zoo brute blue | look | car | for door yawn | fair care | whirl nurse letter | shout cow | boy spoil |
|---|---|---|---|---|---|---|---|

*Each box contains one sound but sometimes more than one grapheme. Focus graphemes are **circled**.*

# Green words



take   while   skirt   nose   lead   slide   rage   came   time   little

zoom   bloom   cute   tune   rude   huge   mule   truce   brute   use

Luke   Bruce   Duke   June   Sue   blue

Read in syllables.

mi`nute   acc`use   ex`cuse   res`cue   tatt`oo   ma`roon   list`en

Read the root word first and then with the ending.

rose → roses          chase → chases          shave → shaved

escape → escaping     choke → choking         pounce → pounced

use → used            refuse → refused

<u>sh</u>**ou**<u>l</u>d   w**ere**   <u>th</u>**ere**   ca<u>ll</u>   want   co<u>m</u>e   c**ou**<u>l</u>d   o<u>ne</u>

<u>th</u>r**ou**gh

# Rex to the rescue

## Introduction

*What type of dogs do you like? Do you think people should be able to control their dogs? What would you do if someone else's dog started fighting with yours?*

*Luke has a little dog called Bruce. Bruce is a very quiet and gentle dog. One day in the park a big, fierce-looking dog, called Duke, chases Bruce. Luke is upset and tries to get Duke's owner to control her dog. But she won't listen. So Luke has a plan.*

*What do you think he'll do?*

Story written by Gill Munton

Illustrated by Tim Archbold

# Vocabulary check

Discuss the meaning (as used in the story) after the children have read each word.

| | definition: | sentence/phrase: |
|---|---|---|
| **tattoo** | a pattern made in ink on your skin | The big bloke with the shaved head and the tattoos. |
| **minute** | tiny | Not so much little as minute! |
| **maroon** | dark red/purple colour | This smart lady in the maroon skirt is Sue. |
| **brute** | a bully | "Shoo, you horrid brute!" said Luke. |
| **refused** | didn't want to do something | She refused to listen. |
| **stubborn** | refuse to give in, determined | Rex is as stubborn as a mule. |
| **truce** | end of a fight | I want all the dogs to call a truce. |

*Punctuation to note in this story:*

*1. Capital letters to start sentences and full stops to end sentences*

*2. Capital letters for names*

*3. Exclamation marks to show anger, shock and surprise*

*4. 'Wait and see' dots …*

*5. Apostrophes to show contractions: couldn't*

## Rex to the rescue

This is Luke. The big man with the shaved head and the tattoos.

The little pug with the blue velvet
collar is Luke's dog. His name is Bruce.
Cute, isn't he? Not so much little as minute!

Luke likes to take Bruce to the park.
Bruce chases sticks (well, twigs) and barks
at the ducks, while Luke sniffs the roses or
reads 'Gardening Today', humming a little tune.

This smart lady in the maroon skirt is Sue,

with her dog, Duke.

Duke's a bulldog, a big brute with sharp teeth.


One day last June, Sue took Duke to the park.

Luke and Bruce were there, too.

Sue let Duke off the lead.

Duke sniffed the ground – he could smell dog!

Then he was off, zooming across the grass.

Past the slide, past the roundabout, past the swings,

until he was nose to nose with Bruce.

"Shoo, you horrid brute!" said Luke,

choking with rage.

It was no use, Duke started to growl

and snarl.

Then he pounced on the poor pug.

Sue came running up.

"Kiss Mummy, Dukey darling!" she said.
"He's in a bad mood today.
The postman escaped before Dukey
could bite him."

"That's no excuse!" said Luke. "Bruce isn't used to fighting.
He's only had one fight in his life – and that was with a hamster,
he lost!"

*The next day*

Just as Luke was sniffing a prize bloom and Bruce was having a snooze on his fluffy blanket, Duke came back.

This time, he chased Bruce all round the park.

"I don't want to be rude," said Luke to Sue,

"but that dog should be kept on a lead."

Sue refused to listen.

"Don't you accuse darling Dukey!" she snapped. "Come on, Duke!"

*The next day*

This little girl is Luke's pal, Fran.

This huge brute is

her dog, Rex.

He's a bull mastiff!

Rex is as stubborn as a mule.

So when he spotted Duke – and chased him across the grass, up

the slide, round the roundabout, over the swings and *right into the*

*lake* – Fran couldn't stop him.

"Thank you!" said Luke to Fran.

He stooped to stroke Rex.

"Good boy!" he said.

"I want all the dogs to call a truce.

No more fighting! Okay?"

"Yep!" barked Bruce.

"Yep!" barked Rex.

"Sploosh!" barked Duke,
through a mouthful of green slime.

# Questions to talk about

*Re-read the page. Read the question to the children. Tell them whether it is a* **FIND IT** *question or* **PROVE IT** *question.*

**FIND IT**

✓ *Turn to the page*

✓ *Read the question*

✓ *Find the answer*

**PROVE IT**

✓ *Turn to the page*

✓ *Read the question*

✓ *Find your evidence*

✓ *Explain why*

| | | |
|---|---|---|
| **Page 9:** | PROVE IT | *Dogs are often like their owners.*<br>*In what way is Luke a surprising character?* |
| **Page 10:** | FIND IT | *What does Sue's dog look like?* |
| **Page 11:** | PROVE IT | *Why was Luke cross with Sue's dog, Duke?* |
| **Page 12:** | PROVE IT | *What is Sue's excuse for Duke? Why is Luke worried about Bruce fighting?*<br>*How do you think Luke felt about Sue as a dog owner?* |
| **Page 13:** | PROVE IT | *What was the problem the next day?* |
| **Page 14:** | PROVE IT | *What type of dog is Rex? What does he do to Duke?* |
| **Page 15:** | PROVE IT | *What do the dogs think of Luke's solution?* |

# Questions to read and answer

*(Children complete without your help.)*

1. What is Luke's dog like?

2. What does Duke do to Bruce?

3. Why was Luke cross with Sue?

4. What does Rex do?

5. What is the truce at the end?

# Speed words

*Children practise reading the words across the rows, down the columns and in and out of order clearly and quickly.*

| listen | pounced | gardening | chases | escaped |
|--------|---------|-----------|--------|---------|
| likes | cute | used | rescue | refuse |
| rude | blue | should | only | were |
| want | come | call | one | couldn't |